LEARNING
ADDITION
USING
LEGO® BRICKS

Dr. Shirley Disseler

COMPASS

Learning Addition Using LEGO® Bricks — Student Edition

Brigantine Media/Compass Publishing
211 North Avenue
St. Johnsbury, Vermont 05819
Phone: 802-751-8802
Fax: 802-751-8804
E-mail: neil@brigantinemedia.com
Website: www.compasspublishing.org
www.brickmath.com

ORDERING INFORMATION
Quantity sales
Special discounts for schools are available for quantity purchases of physical books and digital downloads.
For information, contact Brigantine Media or visit www.brickmath.com.

Individual sales
Brigantine Media/Compass Publishing publications are available through most booksellers.
They can also be ordered directly from the publisher.
Phone: 802-751-8802 | Fax: 802-751-8804
www.compasspublishing.org
www.brickmath.com
ISBN 978-1-9384066-6-9

CONTENTS

WHAT DOES IT MEAN TO ADD?

Part 1

1. Build a model of the number 3 using either three 1x1 bricks or one 1x3 brick. Draw your model and label it Set 1.

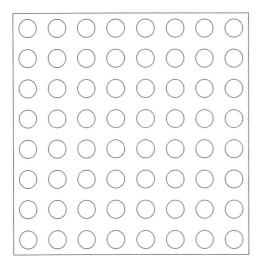

_____

2. Build a model of the number 4 using one of these methods: one 1x4 brick, one 2x2 brick, two 1x2 bricks, or four 1x1 bricks. Draw your model and label it Set 2.

_____

3. What would your model look like if you combined set 1 and set 2?

_____

Draw your solution. Label it Set 3.

_____

Set 3 is called the _____ of sets 1 and 2.

Write the math symbol for this word. _____

Write a math sentence for the action of combining sets 1 and 2. _____

4. Fill in the blank with the correct word from the word bank.

Word bank: set, add, addend, sum

_____: The individual numbers within the problem shown by the studs on the bricks.

_____: The action of bringing together or combining the sets.

_____: The two numbers in an addition problem.

_____: The total of all studs joined together.

5. Build a model of the number 8. Count studs to build your model of 8. The number 8 can be modeled many ways. List some of ways to model the number 8:

_____

_____

_____

6. Build a model of the number 4.

Draw your models of 8 and 4.

7. Draw a box between your drawings of the two sets that show 8 and 4. Place the addition symbol in the box and explain what it means.

The addition symbol means _____

_____

What is the sum? _____

Finish this math sentence: 8 ____ 4 = _____

8. Build a model of 9 + 5 = ⬚ with the following steps:

a. Build the number 9 with studs and draw the model.

b. Build the number 5 with studs and draw the model.

c. Place the appropriate math symbol between the addends in your drawing.

d. Build a model that shows the sum of the two addends and draw the model.

e. Describe your model.

_____

_____

_____

Part 2

1. Can you build a model that shows the number 2 and a model that shows the number 6? Draw your model. Label the numbers *Set 1* and *Set 2*. Build *Set 3* as the sum of Sets 1 and 2. Label the parts of the model and write a math sentence.

2. Can you build a model that shows the number 6 and a model that shows the number 9? Draw your model. Label the numbers *Set 1* and *Set 2*. Build *Set 3* as the sum of Sets 1 and 2. Label the parts of the model and write a math sentence.

3. Can you build a model for this math sentence? 5 + 7 = 12

Draw and explain your model. Label all the parts of the model (addends, sum, math symbol).

_____

_____

_____

_____

4. Can you build a model that shows 2 tens and 4 ones added to 1 ten and 2 ones? What is the sum? _____

Show how you found the sum. Draw and explain your model. Write a math sentence for your model.

_____

_____

_____

_____

Challenge:

Build a model of an addition problem. Do not include the sum in the model. Find a partner and exchange problems. Solve your partner's problem. After you have both completed the problems, discuss your solutions and make sure you can explain the model. Draw your partner's model and your solution to the model. Explain your solution in writing.

_____

_____

_____

_____

Assessment

1. Build a model that shows 2 tens and 3 ones combined. Be sure to show each part of the problem and the solution.

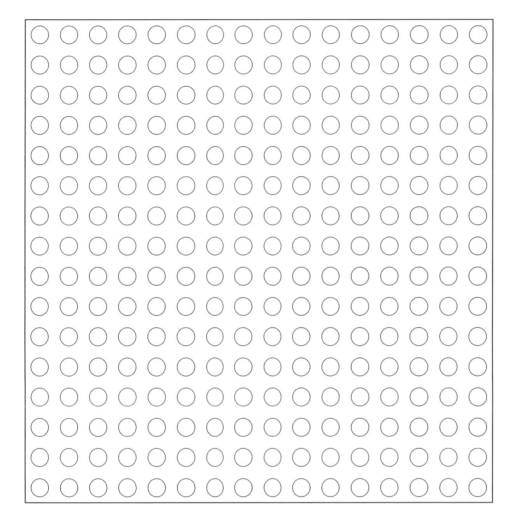

2. Circle the addends in these problems:

8 + 3 = 11

5 + 5 = 10

3. The solution to an addition problem is called the _____.

4. Write an addition problem and model each part of the problem, including the sum. Draw your model.

HOW MANY WAYS?

Part 1

1. Build a base model of 6 using a 1x6 brick.

2. Build a stack model to show all the ways to make the sum of 6. Draw your model.

Write all the math equations you can for your model.

3. Build a base model of 8 using a 1x8 brick.

4. Build a stack model to show all the ways to make the sum of 8. Draw your model.

Write all the equations for the sum of 8.

5. Share your model with a partner and discuss the ways to make 8.

Part 2

1. Can you build a model to show all the ways to make the sum of 4? Share your model with a partner. Draw your model and write all the math equations for your model.

2. Can you build a model to show all the ways to make the sum of 10? Share your model with a partner. Draw your model and write all the math equations for your model.

3. Can you build a model to show all the ways to make the sum of 12? Share your model with a partner. Draw your model and write all the math equations for your model.

Assessment:

1. Build a model to show all the ways to make the sum of 3. Draw your model and list all the equations for the sum of 3.

2. Build a model to show all the ways to make the sum of 9. Draw your model and list all the equations for the sum of 9.

3. Write all the equations for the number 14. Build a model to prove your answer. Draw your model.

3

TEN-FRAMES ADDITION WITHIN TWENTY

Ten-Frame Review:

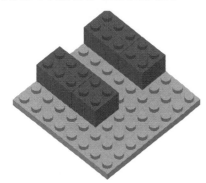

1. Build two ten-frames. Count the number of studs in each ten-frame.

2. Place a 1x1 brick on top of each stud on the first ten-frame.

Draw your model.

3. Place a 1x1 brick on each stud of the top row of the other ten-frame.

How many studs are on that row? _____

Draw your model.

Label your models *Frame 1* and *Frame 2*.

Count to determine which ten-frame models the larger number. Explain how you know.

_____

_____

_____

Part 1

1. Build a ten-frame using bricks that are the same color. Build a model of the number 3 on the ten-frame. Call it *Set 1*, with 3 studs.

2. Build another ten-frame. Build a model of the number 4 on this ten-frame. Call it *Set 2*, with 4 studs.

3. What would the model look like if you combined the studs of both sets?

_____

Write an addition sentence for the model solution.

_____

Draw your model and explain your thinking.

_____

_____

_____

4. Build a model of the number 12 using ten-frames.

On the same baseplate, build a model of the number 8 using another ten-frame.

Build an addition model of 12 + 8 to prove the solution to the problem.

What is the solution to the problem? _____

Draw your model.

Part 2

1. Can you build a model showing the addition of 4 + 6 using ten-frames? Show both sets of numbers and then show how you got the solution with a third model. Draw your models and label all the parts.

2. Can you build a ten-frame model of 14 + 5 and model the solution? Draw your models and label all the parts.

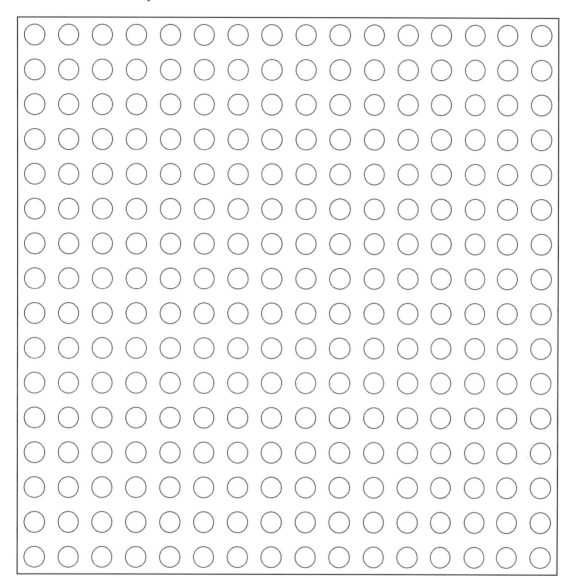

3. Can you build a ten-frame model of 15 + 5 and model the solution? Draw your models and label all the parts.

4. Can you build a ten-frame model of 6 + 6 and model the solution? Draw your models and label all the parts.

Assessment

1. Build a ten-frame model to show 12 + 6 and the solution.

2. Using ten-frames, model two numbers that you could add together to total 14. Draw your model.

3. Using ten-frames, model two different addition problems that have a sum of 18. Draw your models.

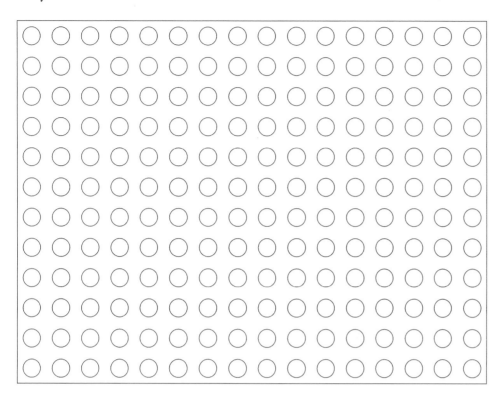

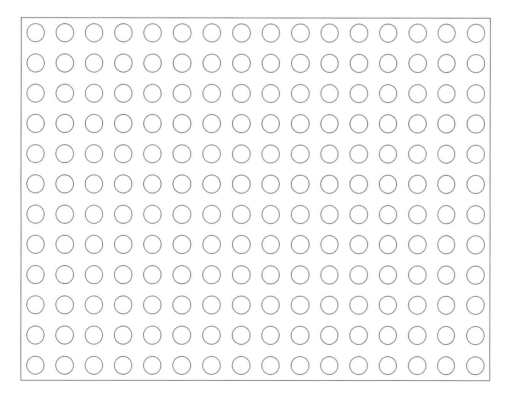

PLACE VALUE ADDITION

Part 1

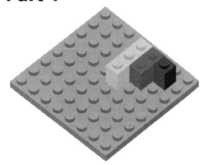

The 1x1 brick represents the ones place because one stud represents one digit (0-9).

The 1x2 brick represents tens because it shows one digit in the tens place and one zero in the ones place.

The 1x3 brick represents hundreds because it shows one digit in the hundreds place and a zero in the tens place and a zero in the ones place.

1. Build the model shown. Draw the model and label each brick that shows the ones, tens, and hundreds place.

2. Build the number 25 using the place value model as a guide. Share your model with a partner and describe the model. Draw your model and explain your thinking.

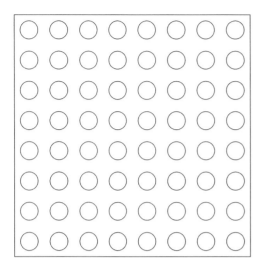

_____

_____

_____

3. Build a model of the number 123 and discuss your model with a partner. Draw your model.

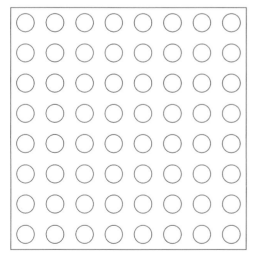

Write the expanded form that the bricks represent:_____

4. Build a place value model for 12 using tens and ones.

Build a place value model for 21 using tens and ones.

Combine the models to show addition.

Draw your models.

5. Use place value modeling to build 25 + 14.

Combine the models to show addition.

Draw your models.

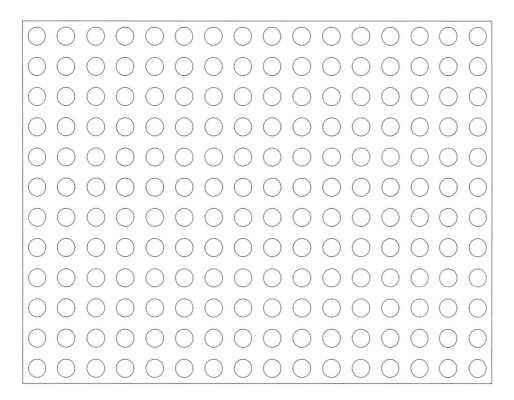

Write the expanded form: _____

Part 2

1. Can you build the number 212 using place value modeling? Draw your model and explain your thinking.

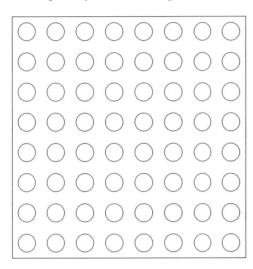

_____

_____

_____

2. Can you build the number 321 using place value modeling? Draw your model and explain your thinking.

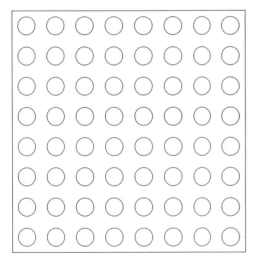

_____

_____

_____

3. Can you build a model that shows the addition of 212 and 321? Draw your model and explain your thinking. Write an addition sentence for your model.

4. Can you build a model that shows 13 + 12? Show all the steps. Draw and explain your model.

_____

_____

_____

5. Can you build a model that shows 123 + 100? Show all the steps. Draw and explain your model.

_____

_____

_____

6. Partner Problem:

Each partner builds a model of a number using place value modeling. Compare your number models. Add the two numbers together. Build a model that shows the addition of both numbers. Draw your model and show your solution.

Assessment:

1. Build a place value model of the number 223.

Draw your model. Circle the bricks that show the number in the tens place.

2. Use a place value model to build and prove the solution for 223 + 55. Draw your model.

3. Demonstrate your understanding of decomposition by building a model of 127 + 134 and the solution.

Show all the steps and explain how you built the solution.

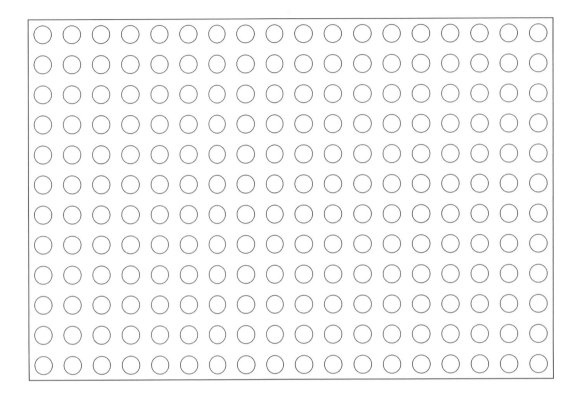

_____

_____

_____

DECOMPOSING NUMBERS

Part 1

1. Build the place value strip model shown using two 1x10 bricks or the equivalent in smaller bricks. Draw the outlines of this model.

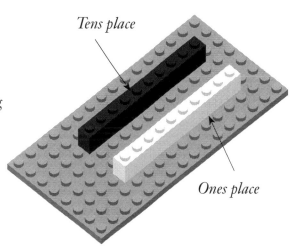

Tens place

Ones place

2. Problem: John has 4 cookies and Samantha has 9 cookies. How many cookies do John and Samantha have altogether?

Write the math sentence for this problem:

_____

These two numbers (4 and 9) are called _____.

3. Model the problem using 1x1 bricks to show the number of cookies each person has.

Choose one color of 1x1 bricks to model John's cookies and select that many bricks. Place these bricks on your baseplate (not on the place value strip model yet). Choose another color of 1x1 bricks to model Samantha's cookies and place these bricks on your baseplate (also not on the place value strip model yet).

Draw your models of the cookies on the baseplate. Label each addend.

4. Move the bricks representing John's cookies to the place value strip model of the ones place. Add the bricks representing Samantha's cookies to the place value strip model of the ones place until you have no more room. What happens when you try to place all the bricks on the ones strip?

_____

_____

_____

5. Trade the ten 1x1 bricks now on the ones strip for one 1x1 brick of a different color. Place this 1x1 brick on the tens strip. Place the rest of the bricks representing Samantha's cookies on the ones strip. Draw your model.

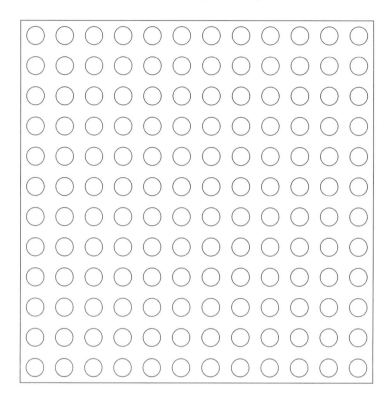

What is the total number of tens and ones in the solution shown on the place value strips?
_____ tens and _____ ones

What is the solution to the problem? _____

6. Problem: There were 8 people in line at the store, then 9 more people got in line behind them. How many people in all were in line at the store?

Write a math sentence for this problem: _____

Select two different colors of 1x1 bricks to represent the addends in the problem. Place these bricks on your baseplate to build models of these addends. Draw the models and label each addend.

7. Build a place value strip model. Move the bricks that represent the number of people in line first to the ones place strip. Add the bricks representing the number of people who joined the line later to the ones place strip until you have no more room on the strip.

What happens when you try to place all the bricks on the ones place strip?

_____

_____

_____

8. Trade the ten 1x1 bricks now on the ones place strip for one 1x1 brick of a different color. Place this brick on the tens place strip. Place the rest of the bricks on the ones place strip. Draw your model.

What is the total number of tens and ones in the solution shown on the place value strips?
_____ tens and _____ ones

What is the solution to the problem?
_____ tens + _____ ones = _____ people in line

This is called _____form.

9. Problem: Savannah had 6 pencils. Christen gave her 7 more. How many pencils did Savannah have in all?

What are the two addends in this problem? _____ and _____

What is the math symbol used to write this problem? _____

What is the answer to the problem called? _____

10. Model the two addends with 1x1 bricks. Build a strip place value model. Show the decomposing of the addends to build the solution using tens and ones. Draw your model. Explain the decomposing of the addends to make tens and ones.

_____

_____

_____

Write an equation to show the solution: _____

Write the expanded form of the sum: _____ tens + _____ ones = _____ pencils

Part 2

1. Build a two-strip model. Can you show the problem 5 + 6 and find the sum using bricks? Write the equation. Draw your model. Label the addends and the sum. Explain how you decomposed the addends to create tens.

_____

_____

_____

2. Steven had 4 pennies and 7 dimes. How many coins does Steven have in all? Build a model to show the total number of coins each person has. Build a model to show the decomposing of the ones to build tens and ones.

Write the equation for your problem. _____

Draw your model and explain your thinking.

_____

_____

_____

Write the expanded form of the sum:

_____tens + _____ones =_____coins

3. There were 12 cars in the parking lot at 6:00 p.m. Five more cars arrived at 6:30 p.m. How many cars were in the lot in all?

Build a strip model and show each addend. Record the two addends: _____ + _____

Build a model to show how to decompose the numbers to create tens and ones.

Write an equation for your model: _____

Draw your model and explain your thinking.

_____

_____

_____

Write the expanded form for the sum:

_____ tens + _____ ones = _____ cars

Assessment:

1. Circle the addends: 6   +   7   =   13

2. Build a place value model of 3 + 8. Show the addends. Show the sum. Draw your model. Label the tens and the ones in the model.

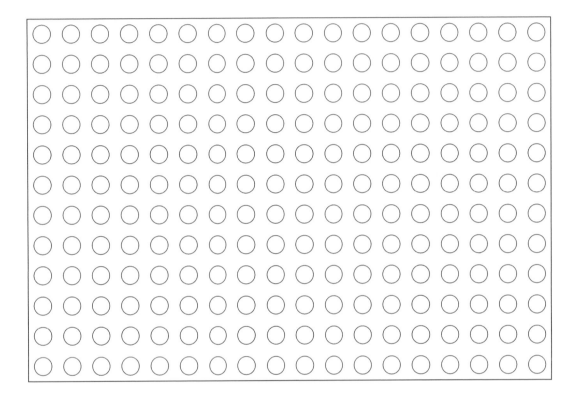

3. Write the expanded form of 14: _____ tens and _____ ones

RESULT UNKNOWN PROBLEMS

Part 1

1. Problem: 2 + 6 = ☐

Think about how to find the missing number that belongs in the box. What is the missing number called? _____

Build three 1x10 number strip models or three ten-frame models to represent the three numbers in the problem (the two addends and the sum).

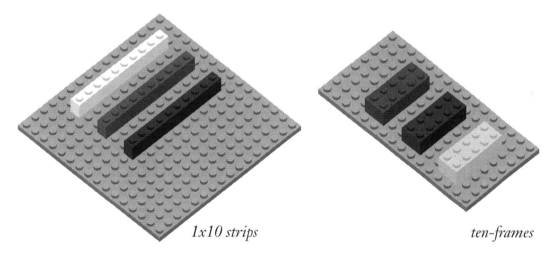

1x10 strips   *ten-frames*

Place 2 studs on the left strip or ten-frame to represent the first_____ in the starting place.

Place 6 studs on the second strip or ten-frame to represent the addend in the _____ location.

Don't place any studs on last strip or ten-frame. This represents the missing _____ .

Find the missing number (the sum) using addition strategies.

Write the math sentence and draw a picture of the addends and the sum. Label each part of the problem.

_____

_____

_____

2. Problem: 3 + 6 = ☐

Build three 1x10 number strip models or three ten-frame models to represent the three numbers in the problem (the two addends and the sum).

Add studs to your model to show the two addends in the problem.

Show the sum.

Draw your model, label the parts, and explain how you found the sum.

_____

_____

_____

3. Problem: 2 + 8 = ☐

Build either a ten-frame model or a 1x10 strip model.

Using this model, add studs to show the addends in the math sentence.

Draw your model of the addends.

How can you find the sum of this math sentence?

_____

_____

Model the sum and draw your model. What are the parts and what is the whole?

Parts:_____ Whole:_____

Part 2

1. Can you build a model that shows this math sentence? 5 + 4 = ☐

Use either a 1x10 strip model or a ten-frame model. Draw your model and show each part of the whole.

What is the sum? Explain how you proved it with your model.

Label each part of the math sentence using the terms *addend* and *sum*.

_____

_____

_____

2. Can you build a model that shows this math sentence? 9 + 1 = ☐

Use either a 1x10 strip model or a ten-frame model. Draw your model and show each part of the whole.

What is the sum? Explain how you proved it with your model.

Label each part of the math sentence using the terms *addend* and *sum*.

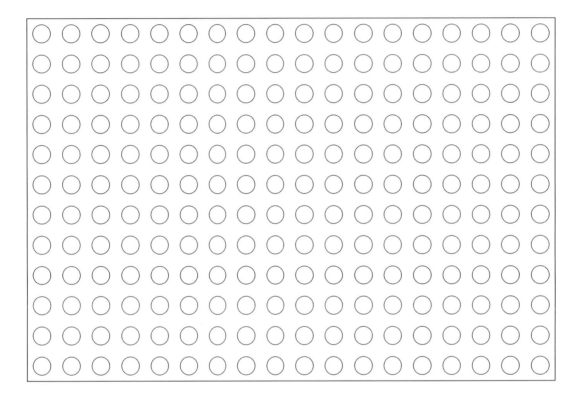

_____

_____

_____

3. Can you build a model that shows this math sentence? 3 + 5 = ☐

Use either a 1x10 strip model or a ten-frame model. Draw your model and show each part of the whole.

What is the sum? Explain how you proved it with your model.

Label each part of the math sentence using the terms *addend* and *sum*.

_____

_____

_____

Challenge:

Build a model to show 5 + 6 = ☐

Hint: You will need more than a 1x10 strip or ten-frame model.

Draw your model and explain how the model proves your solution.

_____

_____

_____

Assessment:

1. The result in an addition problem is called the _____.

2. Build a model for this problem: 4 + 4 = ☐

Draw your model. Label the addends and the sum.

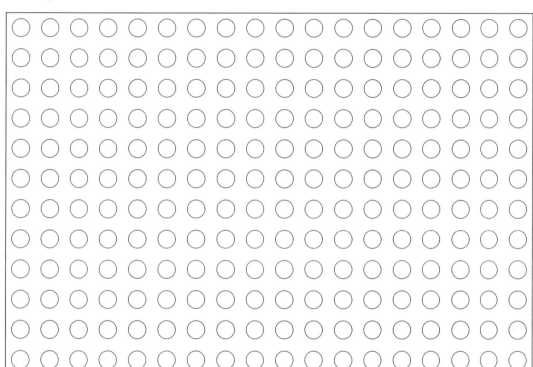

_____

_____

_____

3. Build a model for this problem: 4 + 7 = ☐

Draw your model. Label the addends and the sum.

_____

_____

_____

CHANGE UNKNOWN PROBLEMS

Part 1

1. Problem: 4 + ⬜ = 7

Think about how to find the missing number (addend) that belongs in the box. Build three 1x10 number strip models or three ten-frame models to represent the three numbers in the problem (the two addends and the sum).

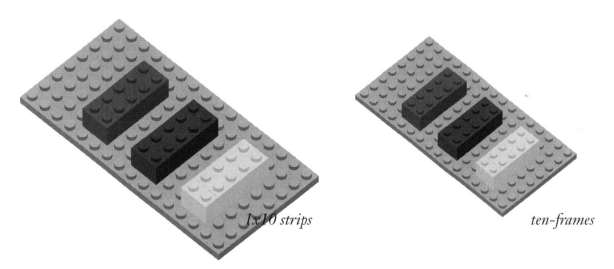

1x10 strips   *ten-frames*

On the left strip or ten-frame, place 4 studs to represent the _____ in the starting location.

On the center strip or ten-frame, do not place any studs. This represents no number in the _____ location.

On the right strip or ten-frame, place 7 studs to represent the_____.

Find the missing number (addend) using addition strategies. Hint: use strategies like counting up, one-to-one correspondence, or matching to find the solution.

Show how you can use comparisons of the two numbers in the problem to find the missing addend.

Draw the model. Label it and explain the parts of the problem.

_____

_____

_____

2. Problem: 5 + ☐ = 9

Build three 1x10 number strip models or three ten-frame models to represent the three numbers in the problem (the two addends and the sum).

Build a model that shows the math sentence.

Model how to find the solution, which is the missing addend.

Draw the model and explain your solution. Be sure to show both addends and the sum in your model.

_____

_____

_____

3. Problem: 2 + ☐ = 8

Build three 1x10 number strip models or three ten-frame models to represent the three numbers in the problem (the two addends and the sum).

Build a model that shows the math sentence.

Model how to find the solution, which is the missing addend.

Draw the model and explain your solution. Be sure to show both addends and the sum in your model.

_____

_____

_____

Part 2

1. Can you model this problem? 3 + ☐ = 5

Step 1: Build the model frame. Use either a 1x10 strip model or a ten-frame model. Draw the outline of the frame.

Step 2: Model the addend (3) and the sum (5). Draw the model.

Step 3: Show all three numbers in the problem in your model and explain how you found the missing addend.

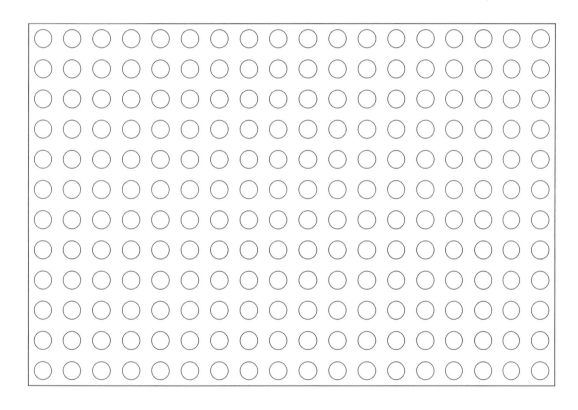

_____

_____

_____

2. Can you model this problem? 8 + ☐ = 10

Step 1: Build the model frame. Use either a 1x10 strip model or a ten-frame model. Draw the outline of the frame.

Step 2: Model the addend (8) and the sum (10). Draw the model.

Step 3: Show all three numbers in the problem in your model and explain how you found the missing addend.

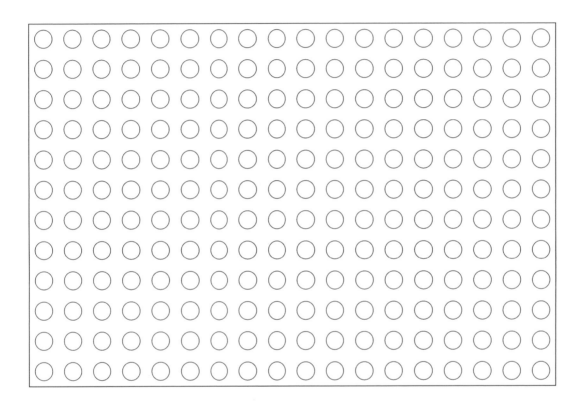

_____

_____

_____

3. Can you model this problem? 4 + ☐ = 7

Step 1: Build the model frame. Use either a 1x10 strip model or a ten-frame model. Draw the outline of the frame.

Step 2: Model the addend (4) and the sum (7). Draw the model.

Step 3: Show all three numbers in the problem in your model and explain how you found the missing addend.

Challenge Problem:

Build a model to show how to solve 6 + ☐ = 13

Hint: You will need more than 10 studs.

Assessment:

1. Circle the addends in this math sentence: 7   +   2   =   9

2. Circle the addends in this math sentence: 6   +   ☐   =   10

3. Circle the sum in this problem: 3   +   4   =   7

4. Build a model that shows how to find the missing addend in this math sentence:

3 + ☐ = 8.

Explain your thinking.

5. Write the math sentence shown in this model. Label the three parts of the problem.

_____

START UNKNOWN PROBLEMS

Part 1

1. Problem: ☐ + 3 = 7

Think about how to find the missing number that belongs in the box. What is the missing number called? _____

Build three 1x10 number strip models or three ten-frame models to represent the three numbers in the problem (the two addends and the sum).

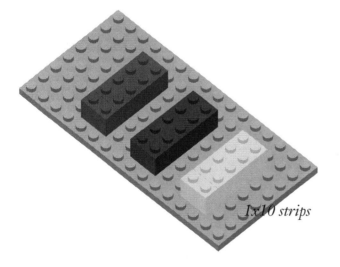

1x10 strips

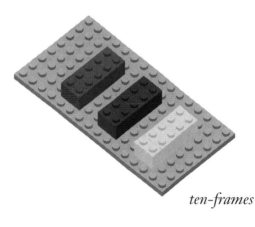

ten-frames

2. Model the problem:

On the left strip, do not place any bricks. This represents no number in the starting location.

On the center strip, place 3 bricks to represent the _____ 3 in the change location.

On the right strip, place 7 bricks to represent the _____.

3. Think of ways to find the starting number using addition strategies such as counting on, one-to-one correspondence, or matching.

4. Compare the two numbers that you know to find the solution. Take 3 more studs that are the same as the ones on the center strip and stack them on top of the 7 studs on the right strip that shows the sum. The number of bricks left uncovered reveals the number of studs needed in the starting location.

5. Model the solution and prove it matches the sum. Draw the model. Label it and explain the parts of the problem.

_____

_____

_____

6. Problem: ☐ + 7 = 10

Build three 1x10 number strip models or three ten-frame models to represent the three numbers in the problem (the two addends and the sum).

7. Model the addition problem by placing bricks on the model to represent the addends and the sum. Then model the addition. Draw and label your model. Identify what each part of the model represents. Show the solution and explain your thinking.

Part 2

1. Can you model and solve this problem? ☐ + 4 = 6

Step 1: Build the model frame. Use either a 1x10 strip model or a ten-frame model. Draw the outline of the frame.

Step 2: Model the addend (4) and the sum (6). Draw the model.

Step 3: Show all three numbers in the problem in your model and explain how you found the missing addend.

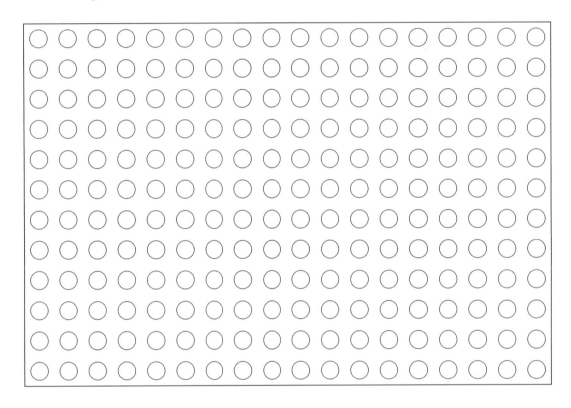

_____

_____

_____

2. Can you model and solve this problem? ☐ + 5 = 8

Step 1: Build the model frame. Use either a 1x10 strip model or a ten-frame model. Draw the outline of the frame.

Step 2: Model the addend (5) and the sum (8). Draw the model.

Step 3: Show all three numbers in the problem in your model and explain how you found the missing addend.

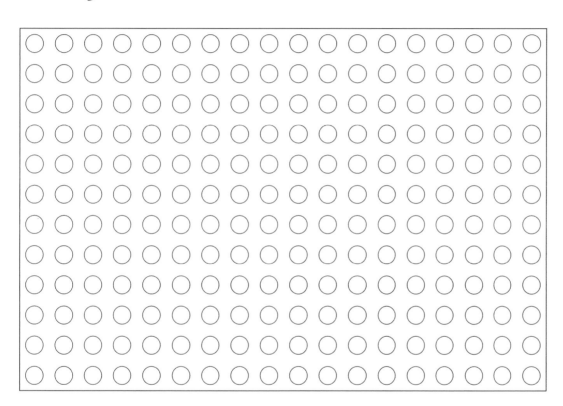

_____

_____

_____

3. Can you model and solve this problem? ☐ + 6 = 9

Step 1: Build the model frame. Use either a 1x10 strip model or a ten-frame model. Draw the outline of the frame

Step 2: Model the addend (6) and the sum (9). Draw the model.

Step 3: Show all three numbers in the problem in your model and explain how you found the missing addend.

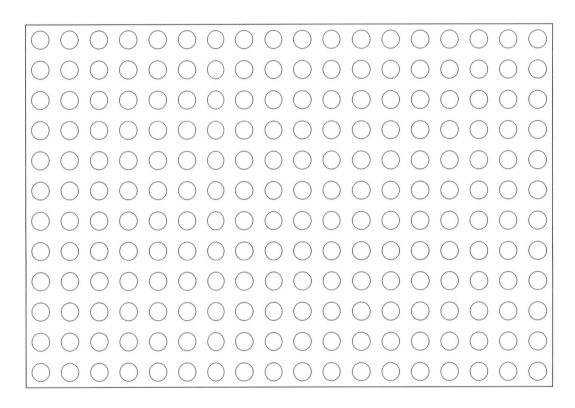

_____

_____

_____

Assessment:

1. Fill in the blanks for the addends and the sum for each math sentence.

$4 + 2 = 6$ Addend _____   Addend _____   Sum_____

$6 + 3 = 9$ Addend _____   Addend_____   Sum _____

2. Build a model to show the problem: ☐ $+\ 4 = 9$

Draw your model. Label each part of the problem as addend or sum.

3. Build a model: ☐ + 4 = 5

Draw your model and show how to find the start unknown number.

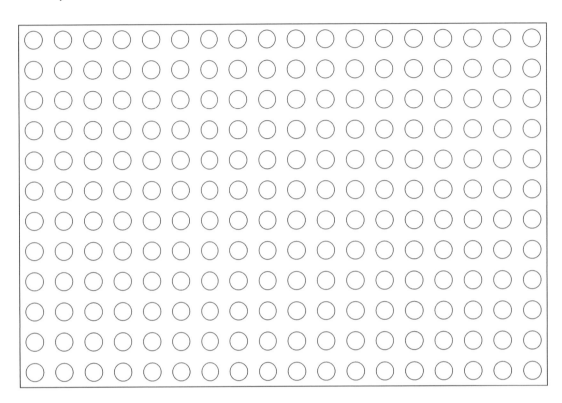

_____

_____

_____

4. Write a math sentence for this model. Without building a model, use a comparison to find the start unknown number.

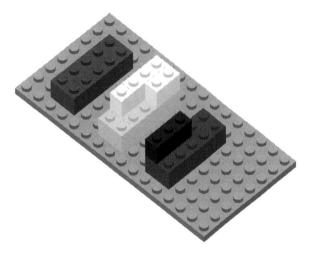

_____

ADDING LARGER NUMBERS

Part 1

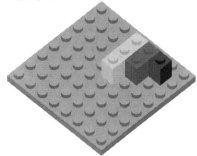

1. Place value modeling review: The 1x1 brick represents ones, the 1x2 brick represents the tens, and the 1x3 brick represents the hundreds.

2. Build the number 22 using two 1x2 bricks and two 1x1 bricks.

Build the number 11 using one 1x2 brick and one 1x1 brick. Draw both models.

<table>
<tr><td>○ ○ ○ ○ ○ ○ ○ ○</td></tr>
<tr><td>○ ○ ○ ○ ○ ○ ○ ○</td></tr>
<tr><td>○ ○ ○ ○ ○ ○ ○ ○</td></tr>
<tr><td>○ ○ ○ ○ ○ ○ ○ ○</td></tr>
<tr><td>○ ○ ○ ○ ○ ○ ○ ○</td></tr>
<tr><td>○ ○ ○ ○ ○ ○ ○ ○</td></tr>
<tr><td>○ ○ ○ ○ ○ ○ ○ ○</td></tr>
<tr><td>○ ○ ○ ○ ○ ○ ○ ○</td></tr>
</table>

3. Build a model that shows the solution of 22 and 11 joined together. Draw the model.

Label the bricks that show the tens and the ones in the solution model.

This model represents 22 + 11 = _____. The solution is called the _____.

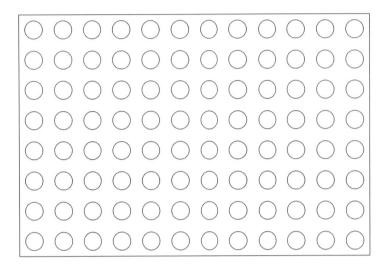

4. Build this math sentence: 35 + 21 = ☐

Build each number, then combine the two addends to form or compose the sum. Draw the solution. Explain your model.

_____

_____

_____

5. Build this math sentence: 62 + 24 = ☐

Build each of the addends, then compose the bricks to form the sum. Draw the solution. Explain your model.

_____

_____

_____

Part 2

1. Can you build a model to show the addition of 33 + 44? Build a model of the sum. Draw and label the model.

2. Can you build a model to show the addition of 56 + 33? Build a model of the sum. Draw and label the model.

3. Can you build a model to show 41 + 36? Build a model of the sum. Draw and label the model.

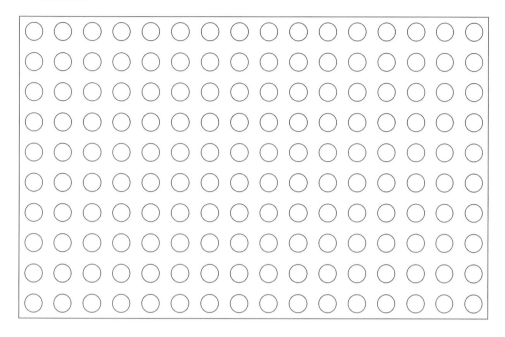

Challenge:

Use what you know about decomposing to find and model the sum of 47 + 38. Build a model, then draw and label it.

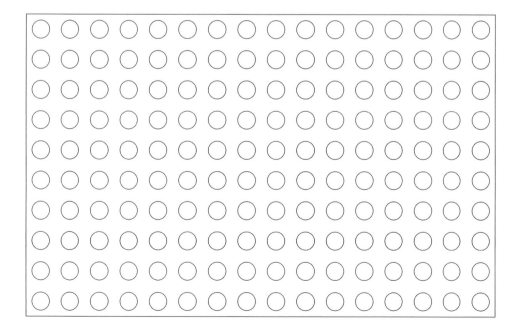

Assessment:

1. The solution to an addition problem is called the _____.

2. Build a model to show the sum of 14 + 43. Draw your model.

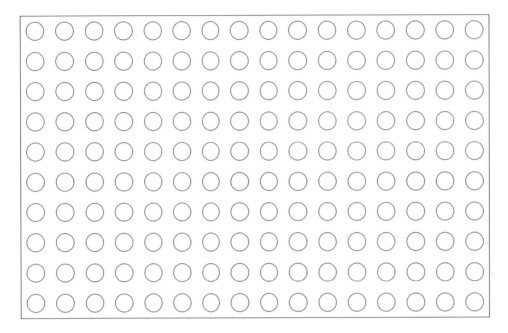

3. Explain what this model shows:

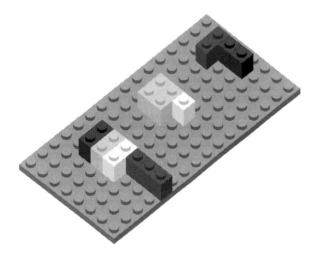

_____

_____

_____

ADDITION
Student Assessment Chart

Name _____

Performance Skill	Not yet	With help	On target	Comments
I can model addition problems using hundreds, tens, and ones.				
I can show and tell what it means to add numbers.				
I can add within 20.				
I can model how to find the first missing addend (start unknown) in an addition problem.				
I can model how to find the second missing addend (change unknown) in an addition problem.				
I can model how to find the missing result in an addition problem.				
I can decompose numbers to make sets of tens and ones.				
I can model many ways to make the same number.				
I can use place value and decomposing to add larger numbers up to 100.				

Brick Math Series:
TEACHING MATH USING LEGO® BRICKS
www.brickmath.com

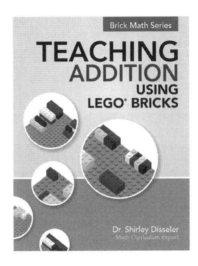

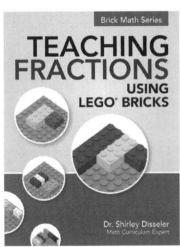

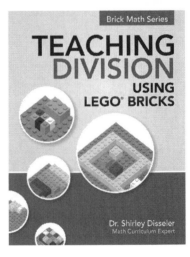

Companion Student Editions

Individual student books that follow the teaching curriculum, complete with additional activities for practice and assessments.

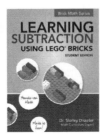

Made in the USA
Columbia, SC
02 May 2021